Jelly Roll Bargello Quilts

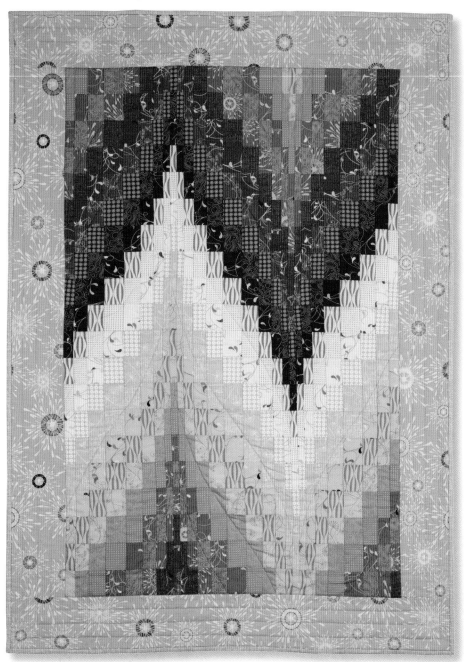

by Karin Hellaby

Landauer Publishing, an imprint of Fox Chapel Publishing

Jelly Roll
Bargello Quilts
by Karin Hellaby

Landauer Publishing is an imprint of
Fox Chapel Publishing Company, Inc.

Copyright © 2018 by Karin Hellaby and
Landauer Publishing, *www.landauerpub.com*,
903 Square Street, Mount Joy, PA 17552.

All rights reserved. No part of this book may be
reproduced, stored in a retrieval system, or transmitted
in any form or by any means, electronic, mechanical,
photocopying, recording, or otherwise, without the
prior written permission of the publisher, except for the
inclusion of brief quotations in an acknowledged review
and the enlargement of the template patterns in this
book for personal use only. The patterns themselves are
not to be duplicated for resale or distribution under any
circumstances. Any such copying is a violation of
copyright law.

Editor/Art Director: Laurel Albright
Editor/Photographer: Sue Voegtlin
Editorial Assistant: Lisa Tetrick
Graphic Designer/Marketing: Catherine Dreiss

ISBN: 978-1-947163-01-0

Library of Congress Control Number: 2018943482

We are always looking for talented authors.
To submit an idea, please send a brief inquiry to
acquisitions@foxchapelpublishing.com.

Printed in Singapore

21 20 19 18   2 4 6 8 10 9 7 5 3

Table of Contents

Introduction

In September 2015, I was preparing projects for a quilting retreat in Assisi, Italy and I wanted one of the project quilts to have an Italian flavor. I considered Bargello to be an exciting option.

Wikipedia states: Bargello is a type of needlepoint embroidery consisting of upright flat stitches laid in a mathematical pattern to create motifs. The name originates from a series of chairs found in the Bargello palace in Florence, Italy, which have a "flame stitch" pattern. Traditional designs are very colorful, and use many hues of one color, producing intricate shading effects.

I first made Bargello quilts 20 years ago as the designs held a fascination for me. How can straight stitches/patches produce an optical illusion of curves? I loved the way a stepped design created vertical zigzag and curved rows.

I find that precut fabrics are always popular on retreats. So why not use a jelly roll and make a Bargello quilt? The wonderful selection of fabrics within a jelly roll would give me the variety required for Bargello patchwork. And best of all, it did not require the effort of finding and selecting 20-40 different fabrics and cutting 2.5" wide strips from each.

The Assisi project quilt I designed proved to be very popular and I submitted it in a proposal to the 2016 Houston Quilt Festival. I was delighted when I was told that this class had over 100 students enrolled. Not only were there many disappointed students who could not get into the class but on social media many asked if there was a pattern or book available. I had no choice but to write one!

Journey with me, as I explain the simplest and most efficient techniques that I have developed to make dramatic Bargello quilts. They will be much admired!

I have traveled to Italy many times both for work and play. It is one of my favorite countries. The idea of naming the projects in this book after places I had visited and writing about why they were so special to me has been a lot of fun, and brought back many happy memories.

Enjoy!
Karin Hellaby

4

Fabrics & Tools

FABRICS

While it's possible to make Bargello quilts by cutting strips from yardage, the ease of using jelly rolls will make your project move along quickly. So much of the work is done for you; fabric is precut and colors from collections already blend well together.

Any 2-1/2" strip collection can be used to make projects in this book but I recommend jelly rolls from Moda or Hoffman Fabrics. Moda jelly rolls have approximately forty 2-1/2" strips by width of fabric and they are from one fabric collection. Depending on how many fabrics are in a collection, every strip can be different or there may be two of each color. Hoffman Fabrics make a pack of 20 strips called Bali Poppies. I have used both of these for projects in the book.

Generally, two sets of 20 strips will make a lap size quilt. When making this size project, the 40 strips are divided and sewn in to (2) 20-strip sets to make the sets easier to handle. Keep in mind that you will need two of each color in a roll of 40 jelly roll strips. Otherwise, you will need to buy two identical 20-strip rolls. Twenty strips will make a wall hanging/crib quilt and 10 strips will make a pillow cover.

TOOLS

Sewing Machine, Sewing Feet and Needles

Make sure your sewing machine is in good working order and you start your project with a new needle. I like to use Microtex size 8 needles for batik fabrics and 10 or 11 for cottons. A larger needle will be needed for quilting.

A 1/4" patchwork foot will help keep your seams consistent. Use a walking foot if you are machine quilting your project.

Rotary Cutting Equipment

The minimum size mat required is 18" x 24". A strip set will sit comfortably on this when cutting the cross strips. A 6" x 24" ruler will easily cover the strip set when cutting. Make sure you have a sharp blade in your cutter for cross cutting the strip set.

Pressing

Use a dry iron when pressing. If there are stubborn creases in the fabric, try spraying lightly with a clear liquid starch such as Mary Ellen's Best Press.

Threads

Aurifil 50wt thread in neutral colors were used for sewing the fabric strips. Aurifil 40wt, which is a bit thicker than 50wt was used for machine quilting.

Marking Pens

Marking pens are only needed for marking quilting lines. A chalk pencil will work or a Frixion pen. Test any marker on fabric first to make sure lines can be removed.

Pins

Use safety pins to mark the start of a strip set and also for marking the corner of your Bargello project. Safety pins can be used to baste the quilt layers together. Fine, sharp quilting pins can be used to pin strips together.

505 Spray and Fix

Spray baste glue can be used to layer quilt layers ready for machine quilting. This is an alternative to safety pins and eliminates the need to remove pins while you are quilting.

Batting

Batting, also known as "wadding" in the UK, comes in different thicknesses, depending on how you want your project to look after it's quilted.

I used Quilter's Dream Poly and Dream Cotton in a 'request' or light weight. Both come in different lofts from lightweight to dense. Lightweight batting is great for hand quilting but if you want your project to be more substantial, try a medium loft batting.

Jelly Roll
Bargello Basics

Please read these basics for a wallhanging/lap quilt before starting your project. Lap quilts, pillows and mini quilts use the same instructions but with different sized strip sets.

1 Open a jelly roll and choose and arrange 20 strips. Use the first 20 or select 20 of your favorites. At this stage you can't plan your finished quilt. As long as you have some contrast, your quilt will be a surprise!

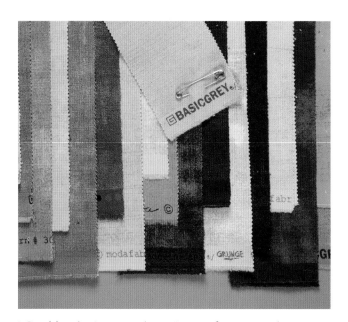

2 Mark the first strip with a safety pin. Set your machine to a small stitch, between 1-1/2 and 2. Sew the first two strips together along one long side using a 1/4" seam.

NOTE: A small stitch keeps fabric from unraveling when narrow cross cuts are made.

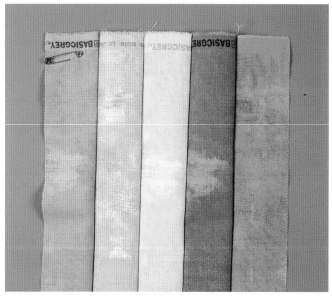

3 Keeping one end of the strip set even, sew the next strip from the opposite direction. (Jelly roll strips can vary in length. If there is a white selvedge on one end, try keeping these on one end of the strip set. The set will be even on one end and less fabric is wasted.) Continue adding strips until you have your first 10 strip set.

4 Repeat with the next ten strips to make a second strip set.

5 Stitch both strip sets together to create a 20 strip set, keeping one end of the set even and seam lines parallel.

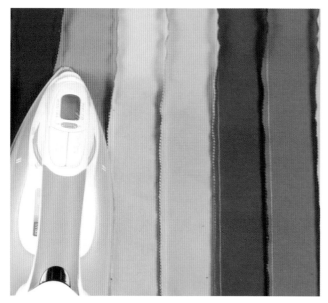

6 Place the strip set perpendicular to the edge of the ironing board. Using a cotton setting, and no steam, press the strip set on the back side. Using the side of an iron, sweep across seams while using your non-ironing hand to gently pull on the seams.

7 Continue pressing until all seams are pressed in the same direction.

8 Turn the set right side up and press while gently pulling on the strip set with your non-ironing hand.

9 Count from the pin on the first strip to find the number 10 strip. Fold the 20 strip set in half, right sides together, along the seam.

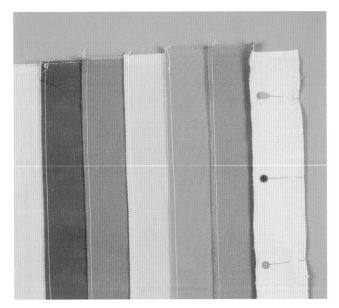

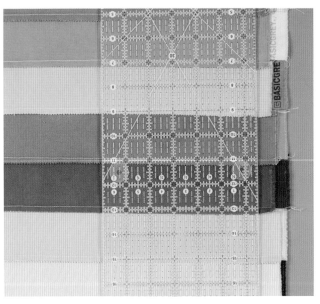

10 Adjust the strip set so the fold is on the horizontal seam line at the number ten seam. Pull gently from both ends of the seam to make the strip set lie flat. Do not try and match sides. Pin the long, raw edges together and stitch into a tube. Press the seam in the same direction as the previous seams.

11 Place the tube flat on a cutting board, right sides together, with seams running horizontally. Place horizontal lines of the ruler along seams and straighten one end of the tube, removing at least 1/2" and making sure there is enough fabric to identify the colors.

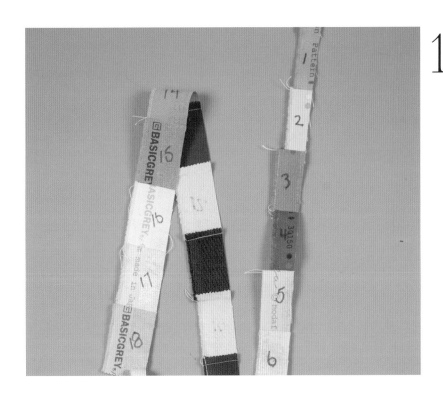

12 Choose any color for the first strip and open loop. Number the cut strip from 1-10, or 1-20, depending on number of strips needed for your project. The strip becomes your reference for where to unsew or cut through a rectangle as you follow steps in a cutting chart.

General Instructions

- When you are ready to start your project, follow these general instructions for either staggered or matched seams.

- Set your machine at a regular straight stitch length before you begin.

- The chart for each project gives you step-by-step information on cut width of strips, where to "un-sew" or cut a rectangle, and what direction the color will move either "up" or "down". As you sew the strips together focus on one strong color and watch it move up or down according to the arrows.

- Use a safety pin to identify the first strip of your project.

- You will be cutting loops starting at the straight edge of the strip set. Attach each strip before cutting the next.

- Use a pencil to check off the row as you complete it. Each project chart has an empty box for this purpose. Use a pencil so you can erase the mark if you choose to make the project again.

- As you sew, make sure you are working with the strip from the correct end. Check by laying each loop alongside the previously sewn strip. This will ensure strips match your pattern and you are un-sewing the right seam or cutting the correct rectangle.

- Approximately half way through a pattern, check that you are still cutting at right angles on the looped strip set. Straighten the edge of the strips if necessary.

Cutting and Sewing the Strips for Your Projects

You are now ready to follow a project cutting chart. Patterns in the book give you the option of either matched or staggered seams. Carefully read the instructions for these two techniques.

How to Use the Chart

"Row" indicates sequential strips in the project.

"Cut Width" indicates width of the strip for the row.

"Open/Cut Strip Between" indicates where to "unsew" a seam or cut a rectangle.

"Position" indicates the direction the colors will flow, either up or down.

Use the last column to **check off** as you finish a row.

ROW	CUT WIDTH	OPEN/CUT STRIP BETWEEN	POSITION	✓
1	2"	1 and 20	Down	
2	2"	Cut 20 in half	Down	
3	1-1/4"	19 and 20	Down	

ROW	CUT WIDTH	OPEN/CUT STRIP BETWEEN	POSITION	✓
1	2"	1 and 20	Down	
2	2"	19 and 20	Down	
3	1-1/4"	18 and 19	Down	

Matching Seams

Matching seams will create a more dramatic design. If you "un-sew" the wrong seam you can easily sew it back together again. Accurately matching the seams will guarantee perfection in the overall look of the design in your project.

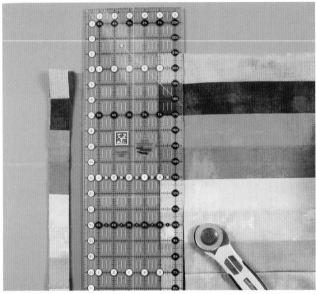

1 Cut the first two loops to the width of your pattern measurements. The first loop and all subsequent loops are un-sewn at a seam line when using the matched method.

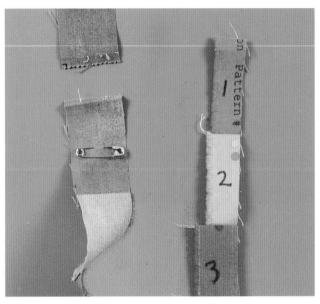

2 Un-sew the loops as directed in the cutting chart. Using the numbered fabric strip, mark the number one fabric of the first cut strip with a safety pin as shown.

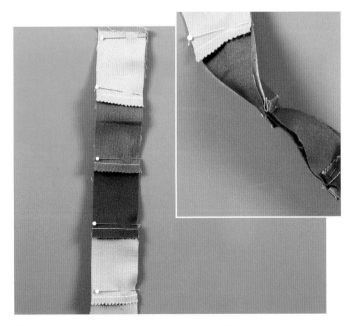

3 Lay the first two strips right sides together and pin the seams in opposite directions. This is the "opposing seam" technique.. (See inset).

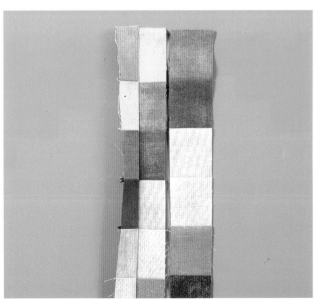

4 Cut and sew the strips one at a time. Lay un-sewn strip next to sewn strips making sure colors are "moving" correctly. Sew strips, alternating sewing direction with each strip through the end of the chart to complete the project.

Staggered Seams

Staggering the seams will create a gentle curve and the strips are easier and more forgiving to sew together. Be sure to concentrate when cutting a rectangle; once cut, it can't be sewn back together!

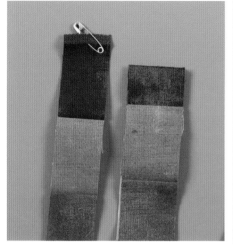

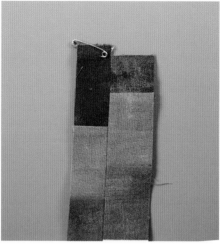

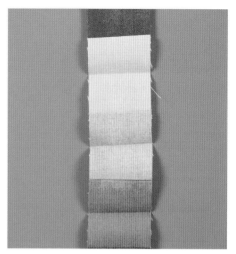

1 Cut the first loop, #1, to the width of your pattern measurement and open at the seam line of your chosen color. Identify the top of this strip with a safety pin.

Cut the #2 loop to the width of the pattern measurement. To make sure you are following the pattern, fold the rectangle in half within the loop and lay alongside the first strip before cutting.

2 Cut across the rectangle and pin the two strips together with the #2 strip 1/4" below #1 strip. The first two strips must be sewn accurately since they are your guide to match subsequent strips.

NOTE: Check twice; cut once. When using staggered seams, it is especially important to cut the correct rectangle in half in each of the **even numbered** strips.

3 Avoid excessive pinning by marking a halfway line on a few rectangles in a strip and use these marks as matching points as you sew.

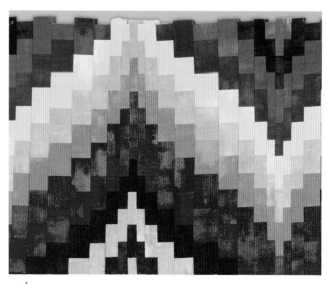

4 The even numbered strips will always start and finish 1/4" off the odd numbered strips.

5 Cut and sew the strips one at a time. Lay un-sewn strip next to sewn strips making sure colors are "moving" correctly. Sew strips, alternating sewing direction with each strip through the end of the chart to complete the project.

Pressing

It is best to press the entire Bargello pattern when it's complete to eliminate distortion. Use the same technique as you did when you pressed strips. (See page 7) Initial pressing is done on the wrong side and final pressing is on the right side of your project.

Trimming Your Project

After pressing, straighten the top and bottom of your project. Stay stitch 1/8" inside all sides to prevent seams from "unfastening".

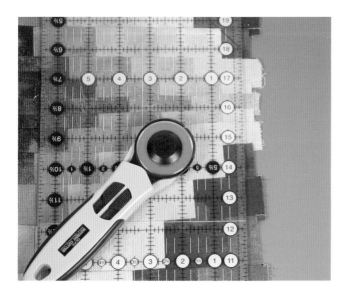

Borders

Most Bargello quilts look best with simple or no borders. You can add binding after layering and quilting your projects.

Quilting
your Bargello Masterpiece!

What You Need to Know

• Press the quilt top well and then trim uneven ends.

• Layer the quilt top with batting and backing fabric. The quilts in this book were layered with a Dream Polyester Request (light weight) or a Dream Cotton Select (light or medium weight). The layers were spray basted using 505 spray or safety pin basted.

• Staggered seams: A marking pen was used to draw a curved line following the center of a fabric or color as it progressed across the quilt. Practice using a chalk powder pen which can easily be erased or a Frixion pen which can be removed using an iron. Once you are happy with the curves you have drawn it is time to machine quilt.

• Matching seams: You may not need to use a marking pen as you simply quilt from corner to corner of a rectangle following the color. The quilting lines will be much straighter.

• I used a Schmetz quilting needle in my machine, usually a size 14 which worked well with 40wt thread. Aurifil 40wt was used for the quilts as the wonderful range of colors were easy to match with the huge variety of colors in the Bargello quilts.

• A walking foot was attached to the machine since it was important for all three quilt layers to stay together when quilting. A straight stitch, a little larger than the regular machine stitch, was used. Practice with a 6-8" quilt sandwich, making sure the tension and stitch length works for you.

• Start stitching from the edge of the quilt, using a needle down position, following the curves towards the peaks and troughs of your design. At these points, stop with the needle down, raise the machine foot and pivot the quilt to work in another direction.

• Once quilting is complete, stay stitch near the quilt edge on all four sides. Trim away excess backing fabric and batting.

• Bind your quilt using your favorite technique.

My favorite quilting for Bargello quilts is to use machine stitched curves. This helps emphasize the optical illusion of curves in the patchwork.

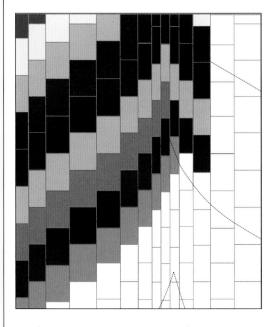

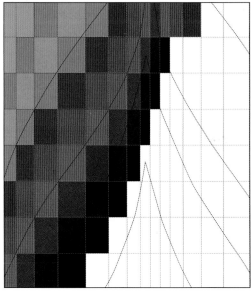

Projects & Charts

What You Need to Know

- This quilt requires two identical sets of 20 strips.
- Choose a 40 strip jelly roll that has two strips of each color or two identical jelly rolls of 20 strips.
- Staggered seams are used.
- Follow Jelly Roll Bargello Basics, page 8, to make strip sets.
- Project instructions and material lists for borders, backing, and binding begin on page 56.

Sorrento

Sorrento is a popular holiday destination near Naples, a place where sea, mountains, citrus groves and deep valleys combine into an extraordinary landscape. Pam's father was here during the war and often spoke about this beautiful place and the Italian family that looked after him.

ROW	CUT WIDTH	OPEN/CUT STRIP BETWEEN	POSITION	✔
1	2"	1 and 20	Down	
2	2"	Cut 20 in half	Down	
3	1-1/4"	19 and 20	Down	
4	1-1/2"	Cut 19 in half	Down	
5	1-1/2"	18 and 19	Down	
6	1-3/4"	Cut 18 in half	Down	
7	2"	17 and 18	Down	
8	2-1/2"	Cut 17 in half	Down	
9	2"	17 and 18	Up	
10	1-3/4"	Cut 18 in half	Up	
11	1-1/2"	18 and 19	Up	
12	1-1/4"	Cut 19 in half	Up	
13	1"	19 and 20	Up	
14	1"	Cut 20 in half	Up	
15	1"	19 and 20	Down	
16	1-1/4"	Cut 19 in half	Down	
17	1-1/2"	18 and 19	Down	
18	2"	Cut 18 in half	Down	
19	2-1/2"	17 and 18	Down	
20	2"	Cut 18 in half	Up	
21	1-3/4"	18 and 19	Up	
22	1-1/2"	Cut 19 in half	Up	
23	1-1/4"	19 and 20	Up	
24	1"	Cut 20 in half	Up	
25	1"	1 and 20	Up	
26	1"	Cut 1 in half	Up	

ROW	CUT WIDTH	OPEN/CUT STRIPS BETWEEN	POSITION	✔
27	1"	1 and 20	Down	
28	1"	Cut 20 in half	Down	
29	1-1/4"	19 and 20	Down	
30	1-1/2"	Cut 19 in half	Down	
31	1-3/4"	18 and 19	Down	
32	2"	Cut 18 in half	Down	
33	2-1/2"	17 and 18	Down	
34	2"	Cut 18 in half	Up	
35	1-1/2"	18 and 19	Up	
36	1-1/4"	Cut 19 in half	Up	
37	1"	19 and 20	Up	
38	1"	Cut 20 in half	Up	
39	1"	19 and 20	Down	
40	1-1/4"	Cut 19 in half	Down	
41	1-1/2"	18 and 19	Down	
42	1-3/4"	Cut 18 in half	Down	
43	2"	17 and 18	Down	
44	2-1/2"	Cut 17 in half	Down	
45	2"	17 and 18	Up	
46	1-3/4"	Cut 18 in half	Up	
47	1-1/2"	18 and 19	Up	
48	1-1/2"	Cut 19 in half	Up	
49	1-1/4"	19 and 20	Up	
50	2"	Cut 20 in half	Up	
51	2"	1 and 20	Up	

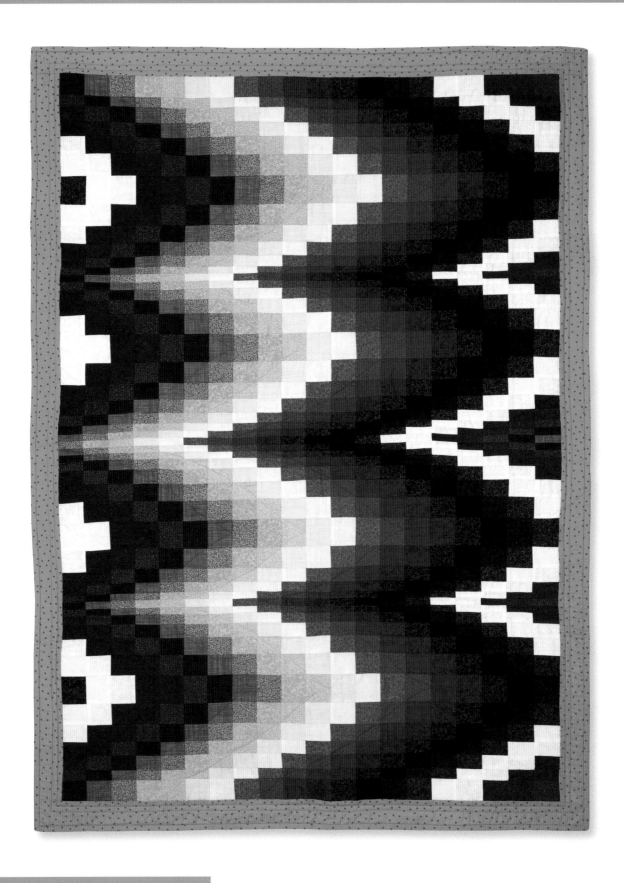

Lap Size Quilt: 40" x 60"
Made by Pam Bailey

What You Need to Know

- This quilt requires two identical sets of 20 strips.
- Choose a 40 strip jelly roll that has two strips of each color or two identical jelly rolls of 20 strips.
- Matched seams are used.
- Follow Jelly Roll Bargello Basics, page 8, to make strip sets.
- Project instructions and material lists for borders, backing, and binding begin on page 56.

Sorrento Seas

ROW	CUT WIDTH	OPEN/CUT STRIP BETWEEN	POSITION	✓
1	2"	1 and 20	Down	
2	2"	19 and 20	Down	
3	1-1/4"	18 and 19	Down	
4	1-1/2"	17 and 18	Down	
5	1-1/2"	16 and 17	Down	
6	1-3/4"	15 and 16	Down	
7	2"	14 and 15	Down	
8	2-1/2"	13 and 14	Down	
9	2"	14 and 15	Up	
10	1-3/4"	15 and 16	Up	
11	1-1/2"	16 and 17	Up	
12	1-1/4"	17 and 18	Up	
13	1"	18 and 19	Up	
14	1"	19 and 20	Up	
15	1"	18 and 19	Down	
16	1-1/4"	17 and 18	Down	
17	1-1/2"	16 and 17	Down	
18	2"	15 and 16	Down	
19	2-1/2"	14 and 15	Down	
20	2"	15 and 16	Up	
21	1-3/4"	16 and 17	Up	
22	1-1/2"	17 and 18	Up	
23	1-1/4"	18 and 19	Up	
24	1"	19 and 20	Up	
25	1"	1 and 20	Up	
26	1"	1 and 2	Up	

ROW	CUT WIDTH	OPEN/CUT STRIPS BETWEEN	POSITION	✓
27	1"	1 and 20	Down	
28	1"	19 and 20	Down	
29	1-1/4"	18 and 19	Down	
30	1-1/2"	17 and 18	Down	
31	1-3/4"	16 and 17	Down	
32	2"	15 and 16	Down	
33	2-1/2"	14 and 15	Down	
34	2"	15 and 16	Up	
35	1-1/2"	16 and 17	Up	
36	1-1/4"	17 and 18	Up	
37	1"	18 and 19	Up	
38	1"	19 and 20	Up	
39	1"	18 and 19	Down	
40	1-1/4"	17 and 18	Down	
41	1-1/2"	16 and 17	Down	
42	1-3/4"	15 and 16	Down	
43	2"	14 and 15	Down	
44	2-1/2"	13 and 14	Down	
45	2"	14 and 15	Up	
46	1-3/4"	15 and 16	Up	
47	1-1/2"	16 and 17	Up	
48	1-1/2"	17 and 18	Up	
49	1-1/4"	18 and 19	Up	
50	2"	19 and 20	Up	
51	2"	1 and 20	Up	

Table Runner: 18" x 43"; Mats (4): 13" x 18"
Made by Karin Hellaby and Pam Bailey

22

Storms Over the Adriatic

What You Need to Know

- The table runner requires a 10 strip set. The same 10 strip set can be used to make four placemats.

- Staggered seams are used.

- Follow Jelly Roll Bargello Basics, page 8, to make strip sets.

- Project instructions and general instructions for borders and binding begin on page 60.

ROW	CUT WIDTH	OPEN/CUT STRIP BETWEEN	POSITION	✓
1	1-1/2"	1 and 10	Up	
2	1-3/4"	Cut 1 in half	Up	
3	2"	1 and 2	Up	
4	1-3/4"	Cut 1 in half	Down	
5	1-1/2"	1 and 10	Down	
6	1-1/4"	Cut 10 in half	Down	
7	1"	10 and 9	Down	
8	1-1/4"	Cut 10 in half	Up	
9	1-1/2"	1 and 10	Up	
10	1-3/4"	Cut 1 in half	Up	
11	2"	1 and 2	Up	
12	1-3/4"	Cut 1 in half	Down	
13	1-1/2"	1 and 10	Down	

23

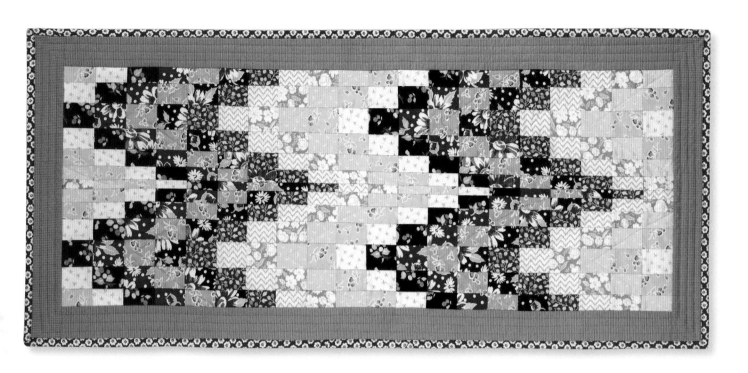

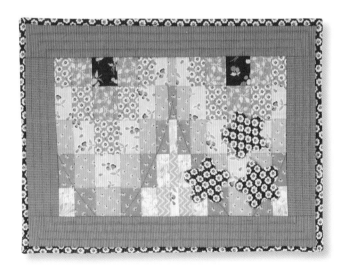 

Table Runner: 18" x 43"; Mats (4): 13" x 18"
Made by Karin Hellaby

What You Need to Know

- The table runner requires a 10 strip set. The same 10 strip set can be used to make four placemats.

- Matched seams are used.

- Follow Jelly Roll Bargello Basics, page 8, to make strip sets.

- Project instructions and general instructions for borders and binding begin on page 60.

Adriatic Beaches

ROW	CUT WIDTH	OPEN/CUT STRIP BETWEEN	POSITION	✓
1	1-1/2"	1 and 10	Up	
2	1-3/4"	1 and 2	Up	
3	2"	2 and 3	Up	
4	1-3/4"	1 and 2	Down	
5	1-1/2"	1 and 10	Down	
6	1-1/4"	9 and 10	Down	
7	1"	8 and 9	Down	
8	1-1/4"	9 and 10	Up	
9	1-1/2"	1 and 10	Up	
10	1-3/4"	1 and 2	Up	
11	2"	2 and 3	Up	
12	1-3/4"	1 and 2	Down	
13	1-1/2"	1 and 10	Down	

Pillow: 20" x 20"
Made by Karin Hellaby

Mount Etna

My first view of Mount Etna in Sicily was of a classic volcano, set against a clear blue sky. This is an active volcano with lava constantly flowing out of the craters, dotted around the mountain.

The closest town is Taormino and this was the venue for a fabulous three-day family wedding in 2008.

We went to the top of Etna to view the lava, a red hot experience on a windy day. At night, the mountain glowed a spectacular backdrop to the wedding celebrations, which I will never forget.

In winter there can be snow on the summit and it becomes a ski resort. Can you imagine skiing on an active volcano?

What You Need to Know

- This project requires a 10 strip set.
- Staggered seams are used.
- Follow Jelly Roll Bargello Basics, page 8, to make strip sets.
- Project instructions and material lists for borders, backing, and binding begin on page 56.

ROW	CUT WIDTH	OPEN/CUT STRIP BETWEEN	POSITION	✓
1	2-1/2"	1 and 10	Up	
2	2-1/4"	Cut 1 in half	Up	
3	2"	1 and 2	Up	
4	1-3/4	Cut 2 in half	Up	
5	1-1/2"	2 and 3	Up	
6	1-1/2"	Cut 3 in half	Up	
7	1"	3 and 4	Up	
8	1"	Cut 4 in half	Up	
9	1"	4 and 5	Up	
10	1"	Cut 4 in half	Down	
11	1"	6 and 7	Down	
12	1-1/2"	5 and 6	Down	
13	1-1/2"	4 and 5	Down	
14	1-3/4"	3 and 4	Down	
15	2"	2 and 3	Down	
16	2-1/4"	1 and 2	Down	
17	2-1/2"	1 and 10	Down	

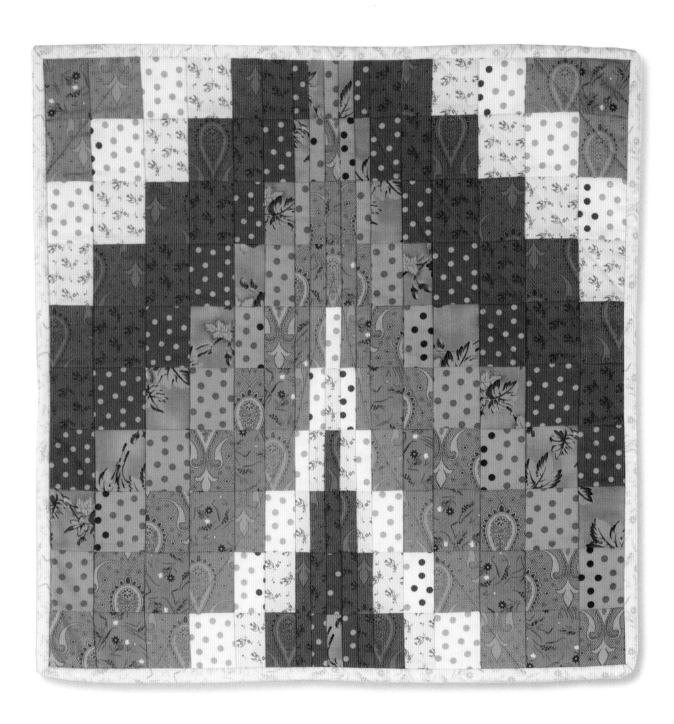

Pillow: 20" x 20"
Made by Karin Hellaby

Erupting Mount Etna

What You Need to Know

- This project requires a 10 strip set.

- Matched seams are used.

- Follow Jelly Roll Bargello Basics, page 8, to make strip sets.

- Project instructions and material lists for borders, backing, and binding begin on page 56.

Lava flows are highly dangerous yet endlessly fascinating!

Mount Etna is one of the most active volcanoes in the world. It is in an almost constant state of activity.

An eruption on the morning of May 13, 2008, immediately to the east of Etna's summit craters was accompanied by a swarm of more than 200 earthquakes. Luckily for us, the volcano was fairly quiet that year for the September wedding.

ROW	CUT WIDTH	OPEN/CUT STRIP BETWEEN	POSITION	✓
1	2-1/2"	1 and 10	Up	
2	2-1/4"	1 and 2	Up	
3	2"	2 and 3	Up	
4	1-3/4	3 and 4	Up	
5	1-1/2"	4 and 5	Up	
6	1-1/2"	5 and 6	Up	
7	1"	6 and 7	Up	
8	1"	7 and 8	Up	
9	1"	8 and 9	Up	
10	1"	7 and 8	Down	
11	1"	6 and 7	Down	
12	1-1/2"	5 and 6	Down	
13	1-1/2"	4 and 5	Down	
14	1-3/4"	3 and 4	Down	
15	2"	2 and 3	Down	
16	2-1/4"	1 and 2	Down	
17	2-1/2"	1 and 10	Down	

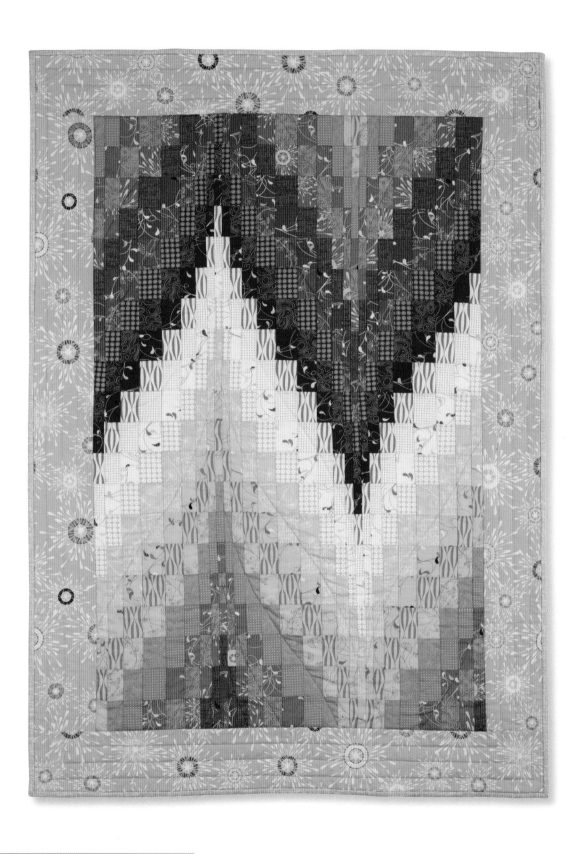

Quilt: 34" x 48"
Made by Karin Hellaby

What You Need to Know

- This quilt requires a 20 strip set.
- Matched seams are used.
- Follow Jelly Roll Bargello Basics, page 8, to make strip sets.
- Project instructions and material lists for borders, backing, and binding begin on page 56.

Venetian Carnival

ROW	CUT WIDTH	OPEN/CUT STRIP BETWEEN	POSITION	✓
1	1-1/4"	1 and 20	Up	
2	1-1/2"	1 and 2	Up	
3	1-3/4"	2 and 3	Up	
4	2"	3 and 4	Up	
5	1-3/4"	4 and 5	Up	
6	1-1/2"	5 and 6	Up	
7	1-1/4"	6 and 7	Up	
8	1"	7 and 8	Up	
9	1"	8 and 9	Up	
10	1"	7 and 8	Down	
11	1-1/4"	6 and 7	Down	
12	1-1/2"	5 and 6	Down	
13	1-3/4"	4 and 5	Down	
14	2"	3 and 4	Down	
15	1-3/4"	2 and 3	Down	
16	1-1/2"	1 and 2	Down	
17	1-1/4"	1 and 20	Down	
18	1"	19 and 20	Down	
19	1"	18 and 19	Down	
20	1"	19 and 20	Up	
21	1-1/4"	1 and 20	Up	
22	1-1/2"	1 and 2	Up	
23	1-3/4"	2 and 3	Up	
24	2"	3 and 4	Up	
25	1-3/4"	4 and 5	Up	
26	1-1/2"	5 and 6	Up	
27	1-1/4"	6 and 7	Up	

Venice is my favorite city. Instead of roads, you see water. I love that!

The history is incredible and it is easy to imagine the beautifully dressed men and women in rich silks, living in the amazing buildings.

I have always wanted to visit Venice at carnival time in February. I can only imagine the elaborate face masks, the bright colors of fabrics and fireworks, as Venice throws off the winter gloom and bursts into life!

Quilt: 34" x 48"
Made by Claire Norman

What You Need to Know

- This quilt requires a 20 strip set.

- Staggered seams are used.

- Follow Jelly Roll Bargello Basics, page 8, to make strip sets.

- Project instructions and material lists for borders, backing, and binding begin on page 56.

Venetian Lagoon

The blues of the Venetian Lagoon and waterways flash with red as the gondoliers row into view. It's a perfect scene from centuries ago to the present day!

ROW	CUT WIDTH	OPEN/CUT STRIP BETWEEN	POSITION	✓
1	1-1/4"	1 and 20	Up	
2	1-1/2"	Cut 1 in half	Up	
3	1-3/4"	1 and 2	Up	
4	2"	Cut 2 in half	Up	
5	1-3/4"	2 and 3	Up	
6	1-1/2"	Cut 3 in half	Up	
7	1-1/4"	3 and 4	Up	
8	1"	Cut 4 in half	Up	
9	1"	4 and 5	Up	
10	1"	Cut 4 in half	Down	
11	1-1/4"	3 and 4	Down	
12	1-1/2"	Cut 3 in half	Down	
13	1-3/4"	2 and 3	Down	
14	2"	Cut 2 in half	Down	
15	1-3/4"	1 and 2	Down	
16	1-1/2"	Cut 1 in half	Down	
17	1-1/4"	1 and 20	Down	
18	1"	Cut 20 in half	Down	
19	1"	19 and 20	Down	
20	1"	Cut 20 in half	Up	
21	1-1/4"	1 and 20	Up	
22	1-1/2"	Cut 1 in half	Up	
23	1-3/4"	1 and 2	Up	
24	2"	Cut 2 in half	Up	
25	1-3/4"	2 and 3	Up	
26	1-1/2"	Cut 3 in half	Up	
27	1-1/4"	3 and 4	Up	

Quilt: 30" x 42"
Made by Beth Ellis

Fluttering Around Verona

Verona, home of Romeo and Juliet is also known for its atmospheric opera venue — a Roman Amphitheatre. This is where I sat with my family, one June evening in 2013, on huge ancient 2000-year-old stone seats, hot from the summer sun, watching my first opera, *Nabucco* by Guiseppe Verdi. It was magical!

ROW	CUT WIDTH	OPEN/CUT STRIP BETWEEN	POSITION	✓
1	2"	1 and 20	Down	
2	1-1/2"	Cut 1 in half	Down	
3	1-1/4"	1 and 2	Down	
4	1"	Cut 2 in half	Down	
5	3/4"	2 and 3	Down	
6	1"	Cut 2 in half	Up	
7	1-1/4"	1 and 2	Up	
8	1-1/2"	Cut 1 in half	Up	
9	2"	1 and 20	Up	
10	2-1/2"	Cut 20 in half	Up	
11	2"	19 and 20	Up	
12	1-1/2"	Cut 19 in half	Up	
13	1-1/4"	18 and 19	Up	
14	1"	Cut 18 in half	Up	
15	1-1/4"	18 and 19	Down	
16	1-1/2"	Cut 19 in half	Down	
17	2"	19 and 20	Down	
18	2-1/2"	Cut 20 in half	Down	
19	2"	1 and 20	Down	
20	1-1/2"	Cut 1 in half	Down	
21	1-1/4"	1 and 2	Down	
22	1"	Cut 2 in half	Down	
23	3/4"	2 and 3	Down	
24	1"	Cut 2 in half	Up	
25	1-1/4"	1 and 2	Up	
26	1-1/2"	Cut 1 in half	Up	
27	2"	1 and 20	Up	

What You Need to Know

- This quilt requires a 20 strip set.
- Staggered seams are used.
- Follow Jelly Roll Bargello Basics, page 8, to make strip sets.
- Project instructions and material lists for borders, backing, and binding begin on page 56.
- Templates on page 62.

Quilt: 35" x 45"
Made by Teresa Wardlaw

Pink Meets Blue in Verona

Shakespeare placed the star-crossed lovers Romeo Montague and Juliet Capulet in Verona for a good reason: romance, drama and fatal family feuding. It's been the city's hallmark for centuries.

A 14th-century residence with a tiny balcony overlooking a courtyard is said to be "Juliet's House." This is where the romantic, but tragic story of boy meets girl unfolds.

ROW	CUT WIDTH	OPEN/CUT STRIP BETWEEN	POSITION	✓
1	2"	1 and 20	Down	
2	1-1/2"	19 and 20	Down	
3	1-1/4"	18 and 19	Down	
4	1"	17 and 18	Down	
5	3/4"	16 and 17	Down	
6	1"	17 and 18	Up	
7	1-1/4"	18 and 19	Up	
8	1-1/2"	19 and 20	Up	
9	2"	1 and 20	Up	
10	2-1/2"	1 and 2	Up	
11	2"	2 and 3	Up	
12	1-1/2"	3 and 4	Up	
13	1-1/4"	4 and 5	Up	
14	1"	5 and 6	Up	
15	1-1/4"	4 and 5	Down	
16	1-1/2"	3 and 4	Down	
17	2"	2 and 3	Down	
18	2-1/2"	1 and 2	Down	
19	2"	1 and 20	Down	
20	1-1/2"	19 and 20	Down	
21	1-1/4"	18 and 19	Down	
22	1"	17 and 18	Down	
23	3/4"	16 and 17	Down	
24	1"	17 and 18	Up	
25	1-1/4"	18 and 19	Up	
26	1-1/2"	19 and 20	Up	
27	2"	1 and 20	Up	

What You Need to Know

- This quilt requires one 20 strip set.
- Matched seams are used.
- Follow Jelly Roll Bargello Basics, page 8, to make strip sets.
- Project instructions and material lists for borders, backing, and binding begin on page 56.

Quilt & Tote Bag: 28" x 41"
Made by Karin Hellaby and Annie Whatling

38

What You Need to Know

- These projects require a 20 strip set.
- Staggered seams are used.
- Follow Jelly Roll Bargello Basics, page 8, to make strip sets.
- Project instructions and material lists for borders, backing, and binding begin on page 56.

Assisi Quilt & Tote Bag

They say that St. Francis of Assisi, born in 1182, would still be able to find his way around his home town. Built on a hillside with narrow cobbled roads and paths, Assisi is a wonderfully atmospheric place. I have taught two quilting retreats here and the quilters have loved sewing on a long balcony with the most amazing views over the plateau below.

This quilt was especially designed for the retreats and uses a Grunge jelly roll by Moda or a bright hand-dyed look.

The stunning tote bag is ideal for carrying your rotary cutting set, with plenty of space for extra rulers.

ROW	CUT WIDTH	OPEN/CUT STRIP BETWEEN	POSITION	✓
1	2"	1 and 20	Up	
2	1-1/2"	Cut 1 in half	Up	
3	1-1/4"	1 and 2	Up	
4	1"	Cut 2 in half	Up	
5	3/4"	2 and 3	Up	
6	1"	Cut 2 in half	Down	
7	1-1/4"	1 and 2	Down	
8	1-1/2"	Cut 1 in half	Down	
9	2"	1 and 20	Down	
10	2-1/2"	Cut 20 in half	Down	
11	2"	19 and 20	Down	
12	1-1/2"	Cut 19 in half	Down	
13	1-1/4"	18 and 19	Down	
14	1"	Cut 18 in half	Down	
15	3/4"	17 and 18	Down	
16	1"	Cut 18 in half	Up	
17	1-1/4"	18 and 19	Up	
18	1-1/2"	Cut 19 in half	Up	
19	2"	19 and 20	Up	
20	2-1/2"	Cut 20 in half	Up	
21	2"	1 and 20	Up	
22	1-3/4"	Cut 20 in half	Down	
23	1-1/4"	19 and 20	Down	
24	1"	Cut 19 in half	Down	
25	1-1/4"	18 and 19	Down	
26	1-1/2"	Cut 19 in half	Up	
27	1-1/2"	19 and 20	Up	
28	2"	Cut 20 in half	Up	

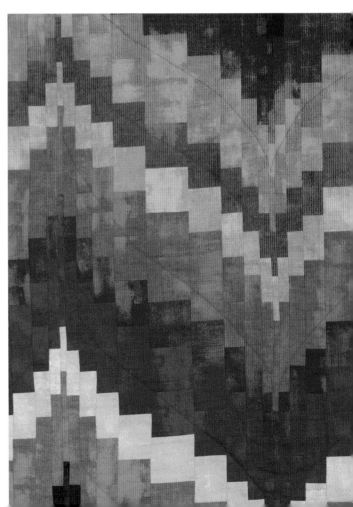

39

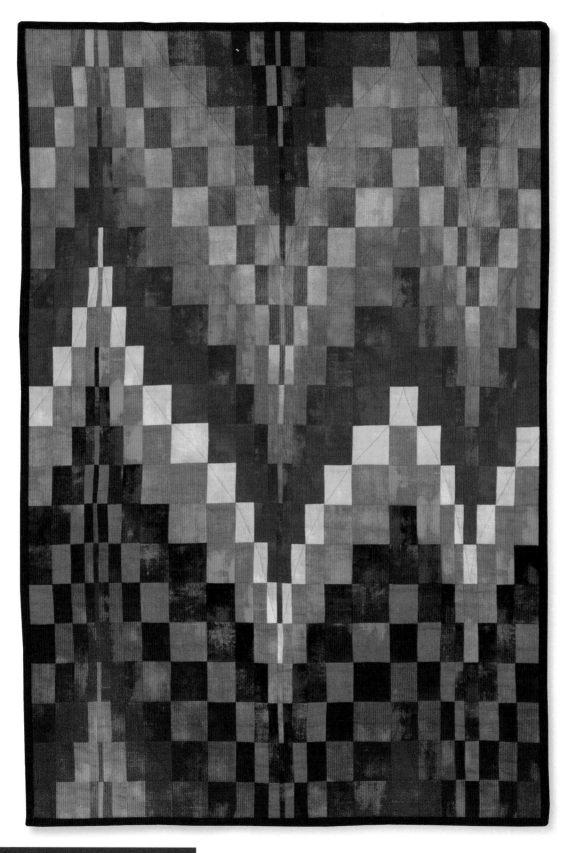

Quilt: 28" x 41"
Made by Annie Whatling

Assisi Quilt 2

ROW	CUT WIDTH	OPEN/CUT STRIP BETWEEN	POSITION	✓
1	2"	1 and 20	Up	
2	1-1/2"	1 and 2	Up	
3	1-1/4"	2 and 3	Up	
4	1"	3 and 4	Up	
5	3/4"	4 and 5	Up	
6	1"	3 and 4	Down	
7	1-1/4"	2 and 3	Down	
8	1-1/2"	1 and 2	Down	
9	2"	1 and 20	Down	
10	2-1/2"	19 and 20	Down	
11	2"	18 and 19	Down	
12	1-1/2"	17 and 18	Down	
13	1-1/4"	16 and 17	Down	
14	1"	15 and 16	Down	
15	3/4"	14 and 15	Down	
16	1"	15 and 16	Up	
17	1-1/4"	16 and 17	Up	
18	1-1/2"	17 and 18	Up	
19	2"	18 and 19	Up	
20	2-1/2"	19 and 20	Up	
21	2"	1 and 20	Up	
22	1-3/4"	19 and 20	Down	
23	1-1/4"	18 and 19	Down	
24	1"	17 and 18	Down	
25	1-1/4"	16 and 17	Down	
26	1-1/2"	17 and 18	Up	
27	1-1/2"	18 and 19	Up	
28	2"	19 and 20	Up	

What You Need to Know

- This quilt requires one 20 strip set.

- Matched seams are used.

- Follow Jelly Roll Bargello Basics, page 8, to make strip sets.

- Project instructions and material lists for borders, backing, and binding begin on page 56.

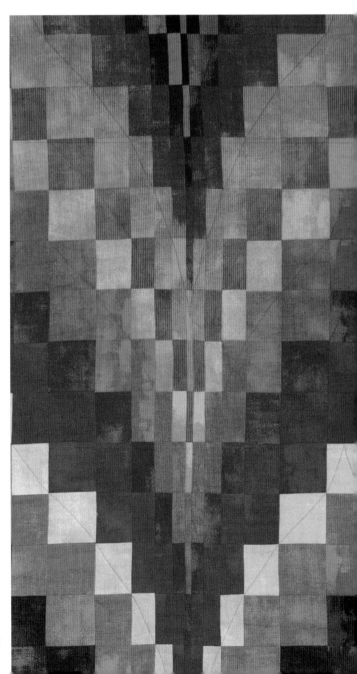

What You Need to Know

- These projects require an 8 strip set.
- Staggered/Matched seams are used.
- Follow Jelly Roll Bargello Basics, page 8, to make strip sets.
- Project instructions and material lists for borders, backing, and binding begin on page 56.

Capri Mini Quilts

Capri is a beautiful island in Italy's Bay of Naples. I spent a day there and it was not enough.

I walked along cliffs that overlooked the deep blue water that laps into secluded coves and mysterious grottoes, passing overgrown sunbleached gardens and beautiful villas.

Next time, I would like to visit the Blue Grotto, a dark cavern where the sea glows electric blue, the result of sunlight passing through an underwater cave.

Staggered

ROW	CUT WIDTH	OPEN/CUT STRIP BETWEEN	POSITION	✓
1	1-1/2"	1 and 8	Up	
2	1-1/2"	Cut 1 in half	Up	
3	1-1/2"	1 and 2	Up	
4	2-1/2"	Cut 2 in half	Up	
5	3-1/2"	2 and 3	Up	
6	1-1/2"	Cut 3 in half	Up	
7	1-1/2"	3 and 4	Up	
8	1-1/2"	Cut 4 in half	Up	
9	2-1/2"	4 and 5	Up	
10	3-1/2"	Cut 5 in half	Up	

Matched

ROW	CUT WIDTH	OPEN/CUT STRIP BETWEEN	POSITION	✓
1	1-1/2"	1 and 20	Up	
2	1-1/2"	1 and 2	Up	
3	1-1/2"	2 and 3	Up	
4	2-1/2"	3 and 4	Up	
5	3-1/2"	2 and 3	Up	
6	1-1/2"	1 and 2	Up	
7	1-1/2"	1 and 20	Up	
8	1-1/2"	19 and 20	Up	
9	2-1/2"	18 and 19	Up	
10	3-1/2"	17 and 18	Up	

I Love Cervinia

It was January 1982, and I was enjoying a two week skiing holiday in Cervinia, a small town high up in the Italian Alps.

Why did I have such a craving for fresh oranges? Was it because high up in the mountains, fresh fruit was difficult to obtain? Why was I nauseous in the mornings? Was it the food?

Back in England I had my first pregnancy confirmed. I knew this was a strong baby who had survived skiing high altitudes at minus eight months. Ross was born the following September and loves skiing, flying from his job in Hong Kong to ski in Japan and Canada.

This book is dedicated to his first child and my first grandchild, who also experienced skiing, at minus six months.

What You Need to Know

- This project requires an 8 strip set.
- Staggered seams are used.
- Follow Jelly Roll Bargello Basics, page 8, to make strip sets.
- Project instructions and material lists for borders, backing, and binding begin on page 56.
- Templates on page 63.

ROW	CUT WIDTH	OPEN/CUT STRIP BETWEEN	POSITION	✓
1	2"	1 and 8	Up	
2	1-3/4"	Cut 8 in half	Up	
3	1-1/2"	7 and 8	Up	
4	1"	Cut 7 in half	Up	
5	3/4"	6 and 7	Up	
6	1"	Cut 7 in half	Down	
7	1-1/2"	7 and 8	Down	
8	1-3/4"	Cut 8 in half	Down	
9	2"	1 and 8	Down	
10	1-3/4"	Cut 8 in half	Up	
11	1-1/2"	7 and 8	Up	
12	1"	Cut 7 in half	Up	
13	3/4"	6 and 7	Up	
14	1"	Cut 7 in half	Down	
15	1-1/2"	7 and 8	Down	
16	1-3/4"	Cut 8 in half	Down	
17	2"	1 and 8	Up	

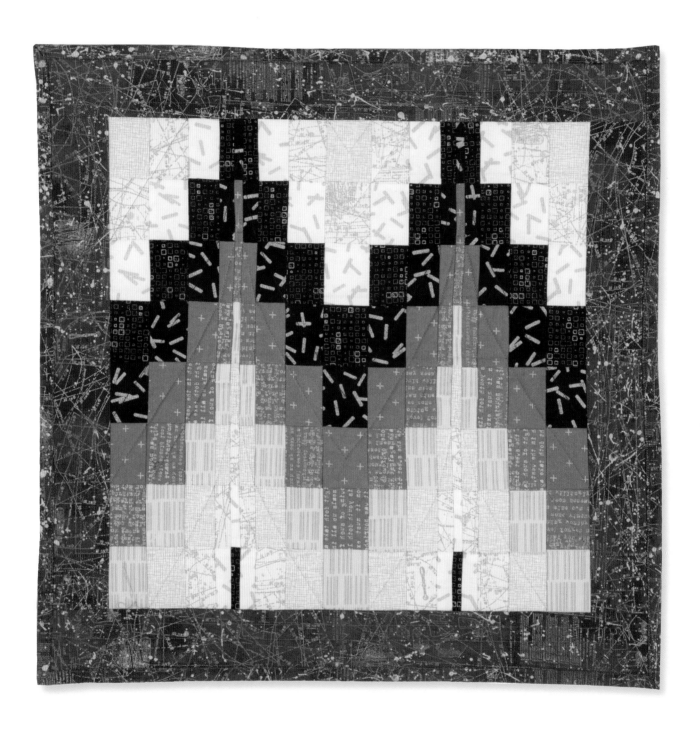

Quilt: 20" x 20"
Made by Karin Hellaby

What You Need to Know

- This project requires an 8 strip set.
- Matched seams are used.
- Follow Jelly Roll Bargello Basics, page 8, to make strip sets.
- Project instructions and material lists for borders, backing, and binding begin on page 56.

Mountain Cervinia

ROW	CUT WIDTH	OPEN/CUT STRIP BETWEEN	POSITION	✓
1	2"	1 and 8	Up	
2	1-3/4"	7 and 8	Up	
3	1-1/2"	6 and 7	Up	
4	1"	5 and 6	Up	
5	3/4"	4 and 5	Up	
6	1"	5 and 6	Down	
7	1-1/2"	6 and 7	Down	
8	1-3/4"	7 and 8	Down	
9	2"	1 and 8	Down	
10	1-3/4"	7 and 8	Up	
11	1-1/2"	6 and 7	Up	
12	1"	5 and 6	Up	
13	3/4"	4 and 5	Up	
14	1"	5 and 6	Down	
15	1-1/2"	6 and 7	Down	
16	1-3/4"	7 and 8	Down	
17	2"	1 and 8	Down	

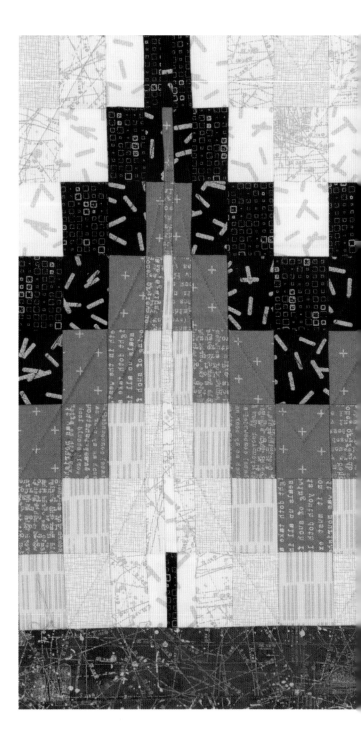

Quilt: 36" x 48"
Made by Marion Barnes

What You Need to Know

• This quilt requires a 20 strip set.

• Matched seams are used.

• Follow Jelly Roll Bargello Basics, page 8, to make strip sets.

• Project instructions and material lists for borders, backing, and binding begin on page 56.

Festive Siena

One of the reasons I love Italy is the food! It is said, 'if you want to eat well, eat Italian'. In Siena, they also say, 'a lunch without wine is like a day without sunshine'. I drink to that!

Many sagre, or festivals, in Tuscany are dedicated around a particular local food. They start in early summer and continue on through the fall as local specialties (truffles, wine, olive oil, marroni chestnuts) come into season.

As well as food festivals, there are religious festivals and Siena has one of the most interesting cathedrals. I visited with a group of quilters and we were amazed at the gorgeous tiled floors with many, many different patchwork designs. This became our inspiration on quilting retreats in Tuscany.

ROW	CUT WIDTH	OPEN/CUT STRIP BETWEEN	POSITION	✓
1	3"	1 and 20	Down	
2	2-3/4"	19 and 20	Down	
3	2-1/2"	18 and 19	Down	
4	2-1/4"	17 and 18	Down	
5	2"	16 and 17	Down	
6	1-3/4"	15 and 16	Down	
7	1-1/2"	14 and 15	Down	
8	1-1/4"	13 and 14	Down	
9	1"	12 and 13	Down	
10	3/4"	11 and 12	Down	
11	1"	10 and 11	Down	
12	3/4"	9 and 10	Down	
13	1"	8 and 9	Down	
14	1-1/4"	7 and 8	Down	
15	1-1/2"	6 and 7	Down	
16	1-3/4"	5 and 6	Down	
17	2"	4 and 5	Down	
18	2-1/4"	3 and 4	Down	
19	2-1/2"	2 and 3	Down	
20	2-3/4"	1 and 2	Down	
21	3"	1 and 20	Down	

Quilt: 35" x 44"
Made by Marion Barnes

Siena Piazza

Piazza del Campo is the principal public space in the historic center of Siena in Tuscany and is regarded as one of Europe's greatest medieval squares. It is one of my favorite places to sit, drink coffee and watch the world go by.

Il Palio is a famous horse race that takes place in the piazza twice a year. For centuries, the horses and their jockeys have ridden the circuit round the campo, overcoming dangerous points where collisions between walls and horses have led to many falls in the past. The first horse past the finishing post after three laps wins, even if he arrives without his jockey.

This quilt depicts the unusual sloping curve of the piazza, the warm tones of the surrounding buildings and a glimpse of cool fountains.

ROW	CUT WIDTH	OPEN/CUT STRIP BETWEEN	POSITION	✓
1	3"	1 and 20	Down	
2	2-3/4"	Cut 20 in half	Down	
3	2-1/2"	19 and 20	Down	
4	2-1/4"	Cut 19 in half	Down	
5	2"	18 and 19	Down	
6	1-3/4"	Cut 18 in half	Down	
7	1-1/2"	17 and 18	Down	
8	1-1/4"	Cut 17 in half	Down	
9	1"	16 and 17	Down	
10	3/4"	Cut 16 in half	Down	
11	1"	15 and 16	Down	
12	3/4"	Cut 15 in half	Down	
13	1"	14 and 15	Down	
14	1-1/4"	Cut 14 in half	Down	
15	1-1/2"	13 and 14	Down	
16	1-3/4"	Cut 13 in half	Down	
17	2"	12 and 13	Down	
18	2-1/4"	Cut 12 in half	Down	
19	2-1/2"	11 and 12	Down	
20	2-3/4"	Cut 11 in half	Down	
21	3"	10 and 11	Down	

What You Need to Know

- This quilt requires a 20 strip set.
- Staggered seams are used.
- Follow Jelly Roll Bargello Basics, page 8, to make strip sets.
- Project instructions and material lists for borders, backing, and binding begin on page 56.

Quilt: 39" x 47"
Made by Karin Hellaby

The Italian Alps

What You Need to Know

- This quilt requires a 20 strip set.
- Staggered seams are used.
- Follow Jelly Roll Bargello Basics, page 8, to make strip sets.
- Project instructions and material lists for borders, backing, and binding begin on page 56.

The Alps are a favorite of mine for walking in the summer and skiing in the winter. They are the highest and most extensive mountain range system that lies entirely in Europe.

Can you believe that Hannibal famously crossed the Alps with a herd of elephants in 218 BC? He guided war elephants from the sunbaked continent of Africa through the snow covered mountains of France and Italy. Imagine the Romans' terror and disbelief at seeing elephants coming down from the mountains, let alone an army of 30,000 soldiers and 15,000 horses! Some of the mountains are steep and jagged while the foothills are more rounded. The quilt below depicts the colors of sunset as night time approaches and Snowy Alps, page 55, shows the drama of wintertime in the mountains.

ROW	CUT WIDTH	OPEN/CUT STRIP BETWEEN	POSITION	✓
1	1-3/4"	1 and 20	Up	
2	2"	Cut 1 in half	Up	
3	2-1/4"	1 and 2	Up	
4	2-1/2"	Cut 2 in half	Up	
5	2-1/4"	1 and 2	Down	
6	1-3/4"	Cut 1 in half	Down	
7	1-1/4"	1 and 20	Down	
8	3/4"	Cut 20 in half	Down	
9	3/4"	19 and 20	Down	
10	1-1/2"	Cut 19 in half	Down	
11	2-1/4"	18 and 19	Down	
12	2-3/4"	Cut 18 in half	Down	
13	2-1/4"	18 and 19	Up	
14	1-3/4"	Cut 19 in half	Up	
15	1-1/2"	19 and 20	Up	
16	1-1/4"	Cut 20 in half	Up	
17	3/4"	19 and 20	Down	
18	3/4"	Cut 19 in half	Down	
19	1"	18 and 19	Down	
20	1-1/4"	Cut 18 in half	Down	
21	1-3/4"	17 and 18	Down	
22	2-1/4"	Cut 17 in half	Down	
23	2"	16 and 17	Down	
24	1-3/4"	Cut 16 in half	Down	
25	1-1/2"	15 and 16	Down	

Quilt: 35" x 46"
Made by Karin Hellaby

What You Need to Know

- This quilt requires a 20 strip set.

- Matched seams are used.

- Follow Jelly Roll Bargello Basics, page 8, to make strip sets.

- Project instructions and material lists for borders, backing, and binding begin on page 56.

Snowy Alps

ROW	CUT WIDTH	OPEN/CUT STRIP BETWEEN	POSITION	✓
1	1-3/4"	1 and 20	Up	
2	2"	1 and 2	Up	
3	2-1/4"	2 and 3	Up	
4	2-1/2"	3 and 4	Up	
5	2-1/4"	2 and 3	Down	
6	1-3/4"	1 and 2	Down	
7	1-1/4"	1 and 20	Down	
8	3/4"	19 and 20	Down	
9	3/4"	18 and 19	Down	
10	1-1/2"	17 and 18	Down	
11	2-1/4"	16 and 17	Down	
12	2-3/4"	15 and 16	Down	
13	2-1/4"	16 and 17	Up	
14	1-3/4"	17 and 18	Up	
15	1-1/2"	18 and 19	Up	
16	1-1/4"	19 and 20	Up	
17	3/4"	18 and 19	Down	
18	3/4"	17 and 18	Down	
19	1"	16 and 17	Down	
20	1-1/4"	15 and 16	Down	
21	1-3/4"	14 and 15	Down	
22	2-1/4"	13 and 14	Down	
23	2"	12 and 13	Down	
24	1-3/4"	11 and 12	Down	
25	1-1/2"	10 and 11	Down	

Project Instructions

GENERAL INSTRUCTIONS FOR BORDERS

Strips for borders are sewn end-to-end when necessary and added to opposite sides of your project. If you choose to miter corners, extra fabric will be needed. Quilt dimensions are approximate.

GENERAL INSTRUCTIONS FOR BINDING

1. Cut strips and sew together end to end.

2. Press seams open.

3. Fold binding strip wrong sides together along the long edge and press.

4. Use your favorite binding method to attach and finish the quilt.

Sorrento and Sorrento Seas

40" x 60"

Border: 1/2 yard: cut (5) 3-1/4" strips

Backing: 3-1/2 yards

Binding: 1/2 yard: cut (6) 2-1/2" strips

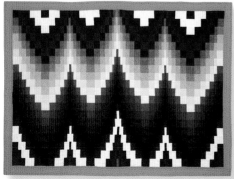

Adriatic

TABLE RUNNER

18" x 43"

Border 1/4 yard: cut (3) 3" strips

Backing: 1-1/3 yds

Binding: 3/8 yard: cut (4) 2-1/2" strips

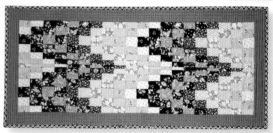

1. Choose 10 strips from a jelly roll and stitch into a strip set, referring to Jelly Roll Bargello Basics, page 8.

2. Straighten both short sides at a right angle to the seams.

3. Measure and cut strip set in half, across the width, at a right angle to the seams.

4. Pin the strips vertically on the short sides so that the color pattern repeats. Sew together with a 1/4" seam and press. You should have about 38"—40" in length and 20" in width.

5. Stitch into a tube and press the final seam in the same direction as other seams.

6. Follow chart cutting instructions to make the table runner top.

7. Press and trim short sides straight, at right angles to the seams.

8. Stitch 1/8" around all edges.

9. Attach borders to quilt top, sewing strips end to end when necessary. Press seams.

11. Layer backing, batting and quilt top. Quilt as desired. Trim edges even with quilt top and bind using your favorite binding technique.

Adriatic

MATS (4 mats)

13" x 18"

Yardage is for four mats

Backing: 1-1/2 yards

Border: 5/8 yard: cut (8) 2-1/2" strips

Binding: 5/8 yard: cut (8) 2-1/2" strips

1. To make mats that match a table runner, choose another 10 strips from runner jelly roll and sew into a strip set, referring to Jelly Roll Bargello Basics, page 8.

2. Trim short sides straight, at right angles to the seams.

3. Measure the length of the strip set (approx. 40") and divide by four. Use this measurement to cut the strip set into four equal sized mats.

4. Stitch 1/8" around all edges.

5. Sew border strips to runner and press seams.

6. Layer backing, batting and mat top. Quilt as desired. Trim edges even with mat top and bind using your favorite binding technique.

Mount Etna and Erupting Mount Etna

20" x 20"

For each pillow:

Backing: 1-1/4 yards
Cut (2) 20-1/2" x 24" strips

Binding: 1/4 yard
Cut (2) 2-1/2" strips

Buttons: (3) buttons

PILLOW TOP

1. Square up short ends at a right angle from seam lines.

2. Cut a 20-1/2" square from the strip set for the pillow top.

3. Sew 1/8" around all edges.

PILLOW BACK

1. Fold each backing piece in half and press.

2. With pillow front wrong side up, align the raw edges of a folded piece with raw edges of pillow front and pin. The fold will face the center of pillow back.

3. Using the second folded backing piece, make three buttonholes, one centered and one spaced evenly on either side of centered buttonhole.

4. Align the raw edges of the piece with raw edges of pillow front and pin in place. This piece should overlap the other backing piece approximately 2-1/2".

5. Sew the backing pieces to pillow front using a 1/4" seam.

6. Attach buttons to fit into buttonholes.

7. Bind the pillow cover using your favorite binding method. Note: The pillow back can be secured with velcro or snaps.

Venetian Carnival and Venetian Lagoon

Approx. 34" x 48"

Border: 5/8 yard: cut (5) 4-1/2" strips

Backing: 1-1/2 yards

Binding: 1/2 yard: cut (5) 2-1/2" strips

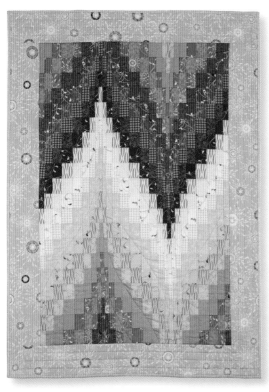

Fluttering Around Verona

30" x 42"

Inner flange border: 1/4 yard; cut (4) 1-1/4" x WOF strips.

Outer border: 5/8 yard: cut (8) 2-1/2" x WOF strips.

Backing: 1-1/4 yards

Inner Flange Border

1. Press strip along length, wrong sides together. Sew a strip to each side of the quilt top, aligning raw edges of folded binding with raw edges of quilt.

2. Layer quilt top, batting and backing. Quilt as desired.

Outer Border

1. There is no batting in the outer border. Sew a strip to each long side of the quit top.

2. With right sides together, sew a strip to top/bottom of quilt top.

3. With right sides together, sew a strip to each long side of the quilt top.

4. With right sides together, sew a second strip to top/bottom and sides of quilt top.

5. Press second set of strips to the back of long sides of the quilt, followed by top and bottom. The seams should lay on the edge of the border.

6. Press 1/4" of border to the wrong side of strip on the long sides of quilt. Hand stitch in place.

7. Repeat for top and bottom border strips to finish the quilt.

Pink Meets Blue in Verona

33" x 45"

Backing: 1-1/3 yds

Border: 1/2 yard: cut (4) 3-1/2" strips

Binding: 1/2 yard: cut (5) 2-1/2" strips

Assisi Quilts and Tote

28" x 41"

Backing: 1-1/4 yards

Binding: 3/8 yard: cut (4) 2-1/2" strips

Straps for tote: 1/4 yard: cut (2) 4-1/2" x 28" pieces

Batting for straps: (2) 1-1/4" x 27" pieces

TOTE BAG

1. Make a wall hanging size quilt completing it with quilting and binding.

2. Stitch the sides together from the top edge to the fold at the bottom, stitching just inside the binding. A zipper machine foot will help you stitch close to the binding.

Handles

1. Cut two 4-1/2" x 21" fabric strips

2. Cut two 1-3/4" x 20" batting pieces

3. Place the batting on the wrong side of each strip, 1/4" away from one long edge. Fold the fabric over the batting and turn under the surplus. Top stitch several rows of stitching onto handles and turn under raw edges on each end of strips. Center and sew handles to each side of tote.

Capri Mini Quilts and Cervinia Mini Quilts

Approx. 20" square

Borders: 1/4 yard: cut (2) 2-3/4" strips

Backing: 5/8 yd

Binding: 1/4 yard: cut (3) 2-1/2" strips

I Love Cervinia and Mountain Cervinia Mini Quilts

Approx. 20" square

Borders: 1/4 yard: cut (2) 2-3/4" strips

Backing: 5/8 yard

Binding: 1/4 yard: cut (3) 2-1/2" strips

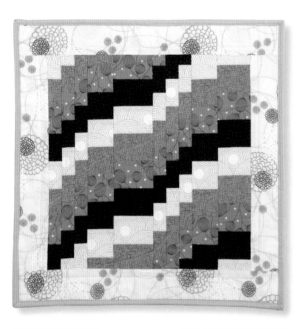

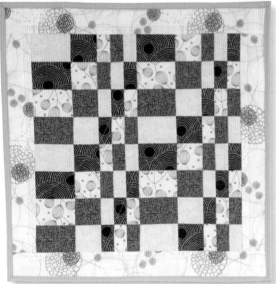

1. Square up strip set to 16".
2. Sew border strips to each side of square.

3. Layer backing, batting and quilt top and quilt as desired.
4. Use your favorite method to bind the quilt.

Festive Siena

36" x 48"

Border: 1/2 yard: cut (4) 4-1/2" x WOF strips

Backing: 1-1/2 yards

Binding 1/2 yard: cut (5) 2-1/2" x WOF strips

Siena Piazza

35" x 44"

Border: 1/2 yard: cut (4) 3-1/2" x WOF strips

Backing: 1-1/3 yards

Binding: 1/2 yard: cut (5) 2-1/2 x WOF strips

Italian Alps

39" x 47"

Backing: 1-1/2 yards

Borders: 5/8 yard: cut (4) 4-1/2 x WOF strips

Binding: 1/2 yard: cut (5) 2-1/2" x WOF strips

Snowy Alps

35" x 46"

Borders: 1/2 yard: cut (4) 3-1/2" x WOF strips

Backing: 1-1/2 yards

Binding: 1/2 yard: cut (5) 2-1/2" x WOF strips

Flutter Around Verona Templates
Cut three birds and 18 leaves

I Love Cervinia Templates
Cut one of each heart

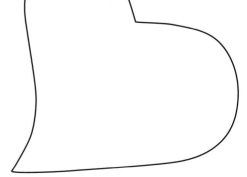

Acknowledgements

Without my band of "merry quilters", this book would not have been completed in time. Pam Bailey, Marion Barnes, Teresa Wardlaw, Annie Whatling, and Claire Norman tested the patterns I designed and made up many of the quilts. I would also like to thank Beth Ellis and Vera Friend who were the first to stitch a jelly roll quilt in Assisi and told me what a great technique this is.

I am also very grateful to my sponsors. Moda and Hoffman, who sent me jelly rolls and fabric. Aurifil, an Italian manufacturer, who provided threads. Quilter's Dream Batting sent poly and cotton waddings. I dealt with all these companies when I had my shop, Quilters Haven, and know their products are the best.

While working on this book I heard that I was going to be a grandmother! I am very excited and knew that I wanted to dedicate *Jelly Roll Bargello Quilts* to my granddaughter, Darcy Freyja. After bringing up three boys, it is wonderful to have a baby girl in the family. I would love to pass on my sewing skills to the next generation and hopefully some of them will enjoy quilting as much as I do!

Other Books by Karin Hellaby

Sew A Row Quilts

Sew A Row Projects

Magic Pillow Hidden Quilts

Fast Flying Geese Quilts

Sew Simple Attic Windows

Sew Simple Pineapple

Pineapple Plus

Sew Simple Pinwheels

Sew Simple Hexi-Flowers